21st Century
Basic Skills
Library

WHAT HAPPENS TO PLANTS IN SUMMER?

by Rebecca Felix

Cherry Lake Publishing • Ann Arbor, Michigan

1

CHERRY LAKE Publishing

Published in the United States of America
by Cherry Lake Publishing
Ann Arbor, Michigan
www.cherrylakepublishing.com

Consultant: Marla Conn, ReadAbility, Inc.
Editorial direction and book production: Red Line Editorial

Photo Credits: Patrick Foto/Shutterstock Images, cover, 1; bst2012/iStock/
Thinkstock, 4; sculpies/iStock/Thinkstock, 6; Shutterstock Images, 8;
Olena Mykhaylova/Shutterstock Images, 10; sonya etchison/iStockphoto/
Thinkstock, 12; Sze Fei Wong/iStock/Thinkstock, 14; kesipun/Shutterstock
Images, 16; GomezDavid/iStockphoto, 18; Zeljko Radojko/Shutterstock
Images, 20

Library of Congress Cataloging-in-Publication Data
Felix, Rebecca, 1984-
  What happens to plants in summer? / by Rebecca Felix.
     pages cm. -- (Let's look at summer)
  Includes index.
  Audience: K to Grade 3.
  ISBN 978-1-63137-603-0 (hardcover) -- ISBN 978-1-63137-648-1 (pbk.) --
  ISBN 978-1-63137-693-1 (pdf ebook) -- ISBN 978-1-63137-738-9 (hosted
ebook)
 1. Vegetation and climate--Juvenile literature. 2. Plants--Seasonal
variations--Juvenile literature. 3. Summer--Juvenile literature. I. Title. II.
Series: Felix, Rebecca, 1984- Let's look at summer.

  QK745.5.F45 2014
  581.7'22--dc23

                                   2014004482

Cherry Lake Publishing would like to acknowledge the work of The
Partnership for 21st Century Skills. Please visit www.p21.org for more
information.

Printed in the United States of America
Corporate Graphics Inc.
July 2014

TABLE OF CONTENTS

4

Sun

Summer is here. Weather is hot. It is often sunny.

The sun shines longer during the day. Sunlight helps plants grow.

Rain

Summer storms bring rain.
This helps plants grow, too.

Plants use sunlight and water to make food. They need food to grow.

Plants grow all summer.
Flowers **bloom**.

What Do You See?

Do you see the pollen stuck on the bees' legs?

Bees

Some flowers have **pollen**.
Bees gather pollen. Young
bees eat it.

Bees **pollinate** flowers. This helps plants to make new seeds.

What fruit do you see?

18

Food

Fruits grow in summer. Many become **ripe**.

What Do You See?

What food is this?

Many vegetables are ready to eat. Fall is coming.

Find Out More

BOOK

Schaefer, Lola M. *Pick, Pull, Snap!: Where Once a Flower Bloomed.* Greenwillow-HarperCollins, 2003.

WEB SITE

Plants for Kids—Science Kids
www.sciencekids.co.nz/plants.html
Learn about plants through games, quizzes, and activities.

Glossary

bloom (BLOOM) to open as a flower

pollen (PAH-luhn) tiny grains made by flowers and used by plants to make new seeds

pollinate (PAH-luh-nate) to carry pollen to different parts of a flower or to another flower

ripe (RYPE) ready to be picked or eaten

Home and School Connection

Use this list of words from the book to help your child become a better reader. Word games and writing activities can help beginning readers reinforce literacy skills.

become	gather	pollen	sun
bees	grow	pollinate	sunlight
bloom	helps	rain	sunny
day	hot	ready	use
during	legs	ripe	vegetables
eat	longer	seeds	water
fall	make	shines	weather
flowers	need	storms	young
food	new	stuck	
fruit	plants	summer	

What Do You See?

What Do You See? is a feature paired with select photos in this book. It encourages young readers to interact with visual images in order to build the ability to integrate content in various media formats.

You can help your child further evaluate photos in this book with additional activities. Look at the images in the book without the What Do You See? feature. Ask your child to describe one detail in each image, such as a food, activity, or setting.

Index

About the Author

Rebecca Felix is an editor and writer from Minnesota. Many types of plants grow there in summer. There are fields of grass and crops of corn. Rebecca likes to pick summer fruits.

24